DATE DUE			

Outlaws and Lawmen of the Wild West

JUDGE
ROY BEAN

Carl R. Green
❯ and ❮
William R. Sanford

ENSLOW PUBLISHERS, INC.
44 Fadem Road   P.O. Box 38
Box 699   Aldershot
Springfield, N.J. 07081   Hants GU12 6BP
U.S.A.   U.K.

Library of Congress Cataloging-in-Publication Data

Green, Carl R.
    Judge Roy Bean / Carl R. Green and William R. Sanford.
       p. cm. — (Outlaws and lawmen of the Wild West)
    Includes bibliographical references and index.
    ISBN 0-89490-591-0
    1. Bean, Roy, d. 1903—Juvenile literature. 2. Texas—
Biography—Juvenile literature. 3. Texas—History—1846–1950—
Juvenile literature. 4. Justices of the peace—Texas—Biography—
Juvenile literature. [1. Bean, Roy, d. 1903. 2. Justices of the peace.
3. Texas—History—1846–1950.] I. Sanford, William R. (William
Reynolds), 1927– . II. Title. III. Series: Green, Carl R. Outlaws and
lawmen of the Wild West.
F391.B328 1995
976.4′06′092—dc20
[B]   94-30108
                                              CIP
                                              AC

Printed in the United States of America

10 9 8 7 6 5 4 3 2

Illustration Credits: Carl R. Green and William R. Sanford, pp. 10, 30; Texas
Department of Transportation, pp. 23, 24, 26, 27, 32; Western History
Collections, University of Oklahoma Library, pp. 7, 8, 19, 28, 35, 37, 39, 41.

Cover Illustration: Michael David Biegel

CONTENTS

AUTHORS' NOTE

This book tells the true story of a colorful saloonkeeper-lawman named Judge Roy Bean. Judge Bean, who dabbled in a number of careers during his lifetime, was as well known a hundred years ago as rock stars are known today. His daring feats appeared in newspapers, magazines, and dime novels. In more recent years, Judge Bean has been featured on movie and television screens. Some of the stories about him have been made up, but many are true. To the best of the authors' knowledge, all of the events described in this book really happened.

1

AN ALL-AMERICAN RASCAL

Judges are supposed to be well-trained, honest, and dignified. Judge Roy Bean of the Wild West was none of these. In the late 1800s Judge Bean ruled his Texas domain like a mischievous, greedy child. Despite his faults, he became a national hero.

Americans have always loved a rascal. Like all great rascals, Roy's life was packed full of colorful escapades. One that made headlines took place in February 1896.

The story starts with a prizefight. At that time many people wanted to outlaw boxing. These people said the sport was cruel and brutal. That objection did not stop promoter Dan Stuart. Stuart arranged for Bob Fitzsimmons to fight Peter Maher for the heavyweight title. The match was to be in El Paso, but Texas quickly passed a law that banned prizefights. Across the Rio Grande, Mexican troops stood ready to keep the fight from moving to Chihuahua. New Mexico Territory was out, too, thanks to a new federal law.

When all seemed lost Stuart received a telegram from Judge Bean. The wire offered Langtry, Texas, as a site for the fight. With the fight crowd growing restless, Stuart checked the railroad timetables. The midnight El Paso train was due to reach Langtry at 1:32 P.M. It just might work! Stuart's return wire told the judge he was on his way.

Texas Rangers moved into Langtry with orders to stop the fight. What to do? From his porch Judge Bean could see the Rio Grande. A remote, unguarded part of Mexico lay just beyond the river. Judge Bean knew the Texas lawmen had no power there. A team of carpenters was soon at work, building a pontoon bridge out to a large sandbank.

The trainload of fight fans chugged into Langtry on schedule. Judge Bean welcomed the thirsty sportsmen. The visitors were happy to pay the outrageous price of a dollar a bottle for Bean's beer. Then the crowd clambered down the riverside cliff and crossed the shaky bridge. A cold rain did not dampen their spirits, nor did the $20 entry fee. Helpless to stop the fight, the Rangers watched from the top of a bluff.

The long-awaited fight ended ninety seconds into the first round. After some aimless sparring, Fitzsimmons hit Maher with a crushing right. The challenger went down and out. With the creaky bridge about to

Judge Roy Bean was around sixty on the day he posed for this portrait (left). He had already lived a full and adventurous life by the time he sponsored the Maher-Fitzsimmons fight. He ordered the construction of this shaky Rio Grande bridge in February 1896 (right). Fans who trooped across the bridge were rewarded with a chance to see a championship fight. Had it not been for Judge Bean's quick thinking, the prizefight would not have been held.

break apart, the fans rushed back up the cliff.[1] Within an hour the train was gone. By the next day the news had spread across the nation. People loved the story of a small-town judge who had outsmarted the government spoilsports. More Roy Bean tales began to circulate. The next story is one of the best.

When trains stopped at Langtry the passengers often left the train to buy a drink at the Jersey Lilly. Judge Bean was napping on the pool table one day when a man

7

rushed in. "Help yourself to a cold bottle," the judge called. The man grabbed a beer and left. In his hurry to catch his train, he forgot to pay for the beer.

Judge Bean strapped on his pistols and ran to the train. Moments later he charged into the smoking car, guns drawn. The passengers froze, certain it was a holdup. When Bean found the man, he roared, "Thirty-five cents for the beer or I press the button!" The man was too scared to argue. He paid.

Bean turned to the other passengers. "If you don't know what kind of *hombre* I am, I'll tell you," he said. "I'm the Law West of the Pecos."[2]

Fight promoters set up a canvas screen around the fight ring. Only paying customers were allowed inside. The screen, however, did little to spoil the view of spectators standing on the nearby cliffs.

2
GROWING UP
ON THE FRONTIER

Roy Bean never revealed the year of his birth. Perhaps he did not know. The best guess is that he was born between 1825 and 1830.[1] His parents, Francis and Anna Bean, lived in northern Kentucky. Later in life, with an eye on his place in history, Roy claimed kinship to Daniel Boone. That may have been one more of his tall tales.

Francis and Anna were backwoods farmers who never owned any land. The Beans do not appear in that era's census records. Some researchers think Francis and Anna raised four boys and a girl.

Later events proved only that Roy did have two older brothers. Joshua was a few years older than Sam, who was born in 1819. Josh, Sam, and Roy grew up thickset and strong.

As a boy Roy learned to swing an ax and handle a

gun. The deer Roy stalked and killed helped feed and clothe the family.

The boy also developed a head for business. He more than held his own when swapping animal pelts for sugar and tobacco. Like Josh and Sam, Roy had little time for book learning. His total schooling added up to little more than three months. He learned to read and write, but not very well.[2]

For Kentucky teenagers a trading trip to New

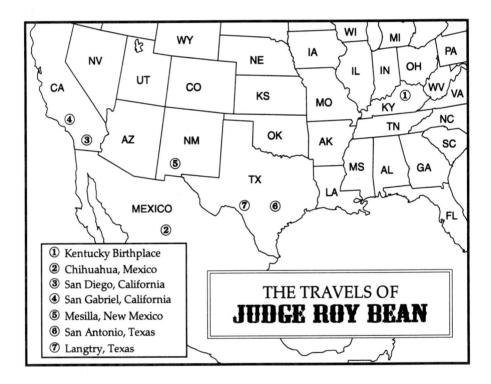

① Kentucky Birthplace
② Chihuahua, Mexico
③ San Diego, California
④ San Gabriel, California
⑤ Mesilla, New Mexico
⑥ San Antonio, Texas
⑦ Langtry, Texas

THE TRAVELS OF
JUDGE ROY BEAN

Judge Roy Bean was born to farmers in the backwoods of Kentucky. He left home with his adventurous brothers as a young man. After stops in Mexico, California, and New Mexico, Roy Bean settled in Texas.

Orleans, Louisiana, was high adventure. After trekking to the Ohio River, they loaded rafts with tallow, tobacco, and whiskey. Strong currents floated the crude rafts downstream to the Mississippi River. From there the great river carried them to New Orleans. After selling their goods the young men helped themselves to the city's delights. Then they set off on the long walk home.

Roy made the trip when he was sixteen. Chances are he enjoyed his first visit to a big city. Perhaps he enjoyed it too much. He stumbled into some sort of scrape and quickly left town. As an old man Roy loved to talk about his travels. In all those tales he never gave the reason for his flight from New Orleans.[3]

One by one Roy's brothers left home. Josh went off to California. Next, Sam headed for Santa Fe. He returned in 1847, an Army discharge in hand. Roy listened with awe to Sam's stories of the Mexican War. He heard about hardships, but he also heard about fortunes to be made. Clearly, men who were tough and ambitious could prosper in the West.

In the spring of 1848 Roy left home with Sam. He never looked back. The first leg of the journey took the brothers to Independence, Missouri. After buying mules, a wagon, and trade goods, they joined a wagon train bound for Santa Fe. From there they took the *Camino Real* south. Sam guessed their trade goods would fetch better profits in Mexico.

The Bean brothers set up a small trading post in the

town of Chihuahua. The locals called them *Los Frijoles* (Spanish for "the Beans"). Roy learned a little Spanish and some Mexican customs. He drank *tequila* and wolfed down *chile con carne*. The relaxed lifestyle seemed to agree with him.

All went well until a *bandido* tried to rob the Beans. The drunken man was waving a sharp knife, but Roy did not back down. Coolly he drew his pistol and shot the would-be robber. His American friends agreed that he had fired in self-defense.

News of the shooting quickly spread. People gathered in the square and heard fiery speakers accuse Roy of murder.[4] Whipped into a frenzy, the mob vowed to kill all the *Yanquis* in town. Warned of the danger, the Beans and their fellow Americans fled northward.

The Beans went to Juarez, Mexico. Sam was in love, and a wedding was being planned. Roy did not stay long. He was too footloose to settle down. The lure of the California gold rush drew him westward.

3
TWO SHOOTINGS
AND A ROPE BURN

Thanks to the 1848 treaty that ended the Mexican War, California now belonged to the United States. Josh Bean gave his brother a bearhug when Roy reached San Diego in 1849. Josh, Roy learned, had become a well-to-do saloonkeeper. A year later the people of San Diego picked Josh to be their first American mayor.

Thanks to his brother, Roy was welcomed into the town's best homes. The local girls lost their hearts to this handsome young man. Major Horace Bell, who knew Roy well, left us a word picture. "His complexion was as fair and rosy as a girl's. Hair black and silky, figure above medium height, and perfect. In manners, a . . . gallant."[1]

In 1851 Josh moved north to open a saloon near Los Angeles. Caught up in San Diego's social life, Roy stayed behind. Soon he fell into a bragging contest with a Scotsman named Collins. To decide who was the better shot, the two men agreed to a contest. Roy, with a wicked smile, suggested they use each other as targets.

The duel on horseback took place on February 24, 1852. After some wild charges back and forth, Roy shot Collins in the leg. A second slug killed the man's horse. As the dust settled, the sheriff stepped forward and arrested both men.

Young Roy Bean found early San Diego much to his liking. Thanks to older brother Josh, he was welcomed into the city's best homes. He might have stayed longer, but the sheriff jailed him for fighting a duel. Roy dug his way out of jail and fled north to San Gabriel.

Young women flocked to the jail with baskets of food, wine, and cigars. Despite their favors, Roy was soon thinking of escape. At first, breaking out of the concrete-and-cobblestone jail seemed impossible. The women solved the problem by smuggling digging tools in their food baskets. Roy dug his way out. Friends had tied his horse behind the jail. The time seemed right to join Josh in Los Angeles.[2]

Roy found his brother in San Gabriel, a few miles east of Los Angeles. Josh put Roy to work behind the bar of his Headquarters Saloon. Business was good. Along with selling liquor, Josh staged cockfights and horse races. Like Roy, he also had an eye for the ladies. That pleasant pastime soon cost him his life.

Legend says that Josh romanced the girlfriend of outlaw Joaquin Murietta. True or not, seven months after Roy arrived, Josh was dead. A bullet fired from ambush ripped through his chest and killed him. A poor cobbler was hung for the crime, but most people blamed Murietta.

Roy took over the saloon. For a time business was brisk. Life turned into one long, sometimes drunken, party. With his black beard and fierce eyes, Roy cut a striking figure. He wore a fine sombrero, embroidered pants, and kept a knife in his boot. Like most of the men he knew, he carried two pistols in his belt.[3]

Once again the good times ended with a shooting. The trouble started in 1855 when a Mexican officer fell for Roy's sweetheart. The would-be lover tried to carry the young woman away, but Roy helped her escape. The frustrated officer then challenged Roy to a duel.

Roy was a better shot than the Mexican—or a luckier one. Either way, he killed his rival. The dead man's friends then took up his cause. They captured Roy and hung him from a tree.

He was dangling in midair when they rode away. The Bean luck was still good, however. The rope stretched enough to let Roy's toes touch the ground. He was still breathing when the young woman arrived to cut him down.

As soon as he could speak, he said, "That's a hell of a way to treat a fighting man. Thank you, sister."[4]

The near-hanging left Roy with a stiff neck. From that day on, unable to twist his neck, he often peered out of the corner of his eye. The odd habit gave him a sly and sneaky look. The rope burn also left a red scar on his neck. For the rest of his life he wore a bandanna to cover the mark.

The brush with death convinced Roy that it was time to move. A few days later he was packed and on the road. Besides, the saloon was losing money.

4
CIVIL WAR
AND WATERED MILK

Roy rode into Mesilla, New Mexico, in 1858 or 1859. He was down on his luck, broke and dirty. His prospects changed when he met the sheriff. The man wearing the star was none other than Sam Bean.

Mesilla, forty miles north of El Paso, Texas, was a lively stage stop. Along with keeping the peace, Sam owned a thriving business. Customers spent their money freely in his all-in-one cafe, hotel, bar, and general store. Roy looked like a saddle bum when Sam saw him. "I got him some clothes, had him shaved and cleaned up, and gave him some spending money," Sam said later.[1] Before long the brothers were partners again.

The boom times ended in 1861 with the coming of the Civil War. Mesilla's townsfolk sided with the South. Roy helped form a freelance group called the Free Rovers. Never a disciplined unit, the Rovers spent their days "liberating" other people's goods. Locals called them the Forty Thieves.[2]

The Free Rovers broke up after a Southern army invaded New Mexico. Many of the men joined the rebel force. Roy hired on as a scout. While on patrol one day he spotted 700 Northern troops camped in a canyon. General John Baylor commanded only 250 men, but he ordered an attack. As they advanced his men raised enough dust to look like a thousand. Thinking they were outnumbered, the Northerners laid down their arms.

In 1862, the Southern forces pulled back to Texas. Roy rode with them. He took with him the contents of Sam's safe, a good horse, and a saddle. Sam could only shake his head sadly. "I never did see much of Roy after that," he said.[3]

A year later Roy opened a freight business in San Antonio. At that stage of the war Northern ships were blockading the Texas coast. Their job was to keep the South from trading with Europe. To get around the blockade, Roy's wagons hauled Southern cotton to Matamoros, Mexico. There at the mouth of the Rio Grande, British ships lay waiting. With the cotton safe in British holds, Sam loaded his wagons with factory goods from Europe. Smuggling, he found, paid good profits at both ends of the journey.

When the war ended Roy was nearly forty years old. He felt it was time to settle down. In 1866 he married eighteen-year-old Virginia Chavez. The couple lived

Judge Bean was a strict but loving father. Four of his children joined him at Langtry after he set up housekeeping in the Jersey Lilly. Here (left to right), Zulema, Sam, Roy, Jr. and Laura take their places with the judge for a family portrait.

south of San Antonio in an area that was soon called Beanville. Virginia gave birth to four children there. The Beans named their sons Sam and Roy, Jr. They called the girls Zulema and Laura. A third son, John, joined the family by adoption.

Flush with wartime profits, Roy wore well-cut suits and smoked fine cigars. At times he worked on the shady side of the law, but few complained. Only a brave man would challenge Roy Bean. When pushed, Roy could outdrink, outbluff, and outswear any Texan around.

Before long Roy's ventures went sour. He was forced to scrounge for every dollar. For a while he sold firewood—with wood cut from another man's land. Next he went into the dairy business. After picking up thirty cows in a swap, he started a milk route. When feed costs soared, he put the herd on short rations. Starving cows give little milk, however. Roy solved the problem by adding water to the little milk they did produce.

One day a local judge knocked on Roy's door. He had found a minnow in his milk, he complained. "By God," Roy swore, "that's what I get for watering them cows down at the river."[4]

After the dairy failed Roy started a meat business. He bought "stray" cows and horses for five dollars each, no questions asked. As always, he was better at borrowing money than he was at paying it back. When he was sued for nonpayment of debts, Roy fought back with lawsuits of his own. The hours he spent in courtrooms gave him a working knowledge of the law.

By 1880 Roy's freight wagons were falling apart. His mules were dying on their feet. He yearned to make a fresh start. West Texas, where the railroads were laying new track, sounded promising. "I'd like to move out to that country," he said. "No law west of the Pecos? Well, God knows, there's too much law around [San Antonio]."[5]

5
A SELF-MADE JUDGE

In the spring of 1882 Roy sold his wagons and mules. The sale netted him $900, which he used to equip himself for his new venture.[1] Then he said goodbye to his wife. Virginia did not want to leave San Antonio. Later, when it was clear that Roy was gone for good, she divorced him and remarried.

Driving a wagon loaded with a tent, a barrel of whiskey, and crates of bottled beer, Roy headed west. Somewhere beyond the Pecos River, the Sunset Railroad was laying track. As the track-laying crews moved west, the railhead towns packed up and followed.

Roy caught up with this traveling sideshow at Vinegaroon, Texas. Named for a local scorpion, Vinegaroon was nothing but crude shacks and sagging tents. It existed to help hard-drinking workers spend their pay. The gamblers and saloon girls spoke of their movable town as "Hell on Wheels."

Laying track through the canyon of the Rio Grande was slow work. Vinegaroon prospered as workmen blasted, tunneled, and graded. Roy pitched his tent at Eagle's Nest, west of town. His saloon was soon doing a lively business. On July 27, 1882, he confirmed his new status by sending a notice to the *San Antonio Express*:

> *A Card from Roy Bean, [of] Beanville . . .*
> *Eagle's Nest Springs, Pecos County . . .*
>
> *I would announce to my friends and the public in general that I have opened another saloon at the above place, where can be found the best of wines, liquors and cigars. . . . Visitors will always find a quiet, orderly place, where they can get a good drink. . . . The water is good and the scenery grand. Will be pleased to see any of my friends at all times.*
>
> *Roy Bean*[2]

A handful of Texas Rangers did their best to police the rowdy railroad towns. Lacking a local court, they had to escort suspects to far-off Fort Stockton for trial. Perhaps railroad officials asked Roy to fill the gap. Perhaps the canny old saloonkeeper saw a chance at fame. In any case, he began calling himself Judge Roy Bean, Law West of the Pecos.

Today's visitors find it hard to believe that Vinegaroon was once a lively frontier town. Only a few ruins remain to mark the site. In the distance, the Rio Grande slips quietly past, just as it did in Roy Bean's time.

Judge Bean held his first trial in July 1882. A month later Pecos County named him a Justice of the Peace (JP). Roy did not know much law, but he talked a good game. The lessons learned in San Antonio's courtrooms were paying off. In September the Rangers set up a post at Vinegaroon. Roy struck his tent and moved along with them. To hold a trial, he simply turned his saloon into a courtroom.

Pecos County did not have a jail. Roy punished the guilty by fining them. The money went into his pocket. After all, he reasoned, a court should pay its own way. Roy also believed that justice should be swift. During one case a lawyer questioned one of his rulings. Roy turned to a Ranger standing nearby. What would you do, he asked, if the court sentenced the lawyer to be hung. "I'd take him out and hang him," the Ranger replied. The lawyer took a look at their grim faces and dropped his objection.

Judge Bean's brand of rough justice saved the county both time and money. Typical was the case brought by a rancher who caught a man stealing a horse. Judge Bean noticed the thief's ear had been nicked by a bullet. "If you could shoot better you wouldn't be wastin' my time," Roy snapped at the rancher.

Then he turned to the accused. "You get the hell out of here. An' don't come back unless you want to get your neck stretched," he ordered. The horse thief did not argue. He took off running, happy to leave Pecos County alive.[3]

Judge Bean's law library held only one volume, the 1879 Revised Statutes of Texas. That book, plus his notary seal, pistol, and handcuffs were all the equipment the old judge needed. The gun, a gift from Lily Langtry, served as his gavel.

6

THE JERSEY LILLY

By the end of 1882 Vinegaroon was shutting down. When calls for his services lagged, Judge Bean moved 70 miles west to Strawbridge (now Sanderson). Charlie Wilson had already opened a saloon there, but Roy did not worry. In a showdown a few well-placed rifle bullets were sure to send the competition packing.

Rather than tackle the judge head on, Wilson hatched a plot. Roy was asleep late one night when Wilson sent a man sneaking into his tent. The first sign of trouble came the next morning. Roy's customers cursed as they spit out their whiskey. The judge took one taste and joined them. The whiskey tasted strongly of kerosene.[1]

Roy knew when to fold a losing hand. He left Strawbridge to Wilson and returned to Eagle's Nest. The site pleased him. Jesus Torres was laying out a small town on land his father owned. In nearby Dead Man's

Canyon, two major rail lines were about to join. Soon trains would be stopping for water. Thirsty travelers would want a cold beer. Best of all the new town needed a Justice of the Peace.

Roy opened his first saloon just south of the railroad right of way. He ignored the fact that the land did not belong to him. Later he moved to a wooden building north of the tracks. Railroad officials were happy to lease the land to Roy. They counted on him to help keep the peace.

Locals were soon calling the town Langtry. Judge Bean wrote to British actress Lily Langtry to say that he had named the town for her. Roy worshipped Lily, who

Not far from this rugged gorge, the Pecos River joins the Rio Grande. Roy Bean settled nearby in a town that became known as Langtry. He was welcome there. Courtrooms and saloons were scarce, and Roy provided both services.

In good weather, Judge Bean sometimes held court on the porch of the Jersey Lilly. In this diorama, Roy is about to pass sentence on a horse thief. The front part of the building served as bar, billiard hall, and general store. Behind lay the family's living quarters and sleeping rooms that rented by the night.

was one of the era's great beauties. He called his new wooden building *The Jersey Lilly*. The name was a second tribute to Lily, who was born on the island of Jersey. A half-drunk sign painter added the extra "l."[2]

Lily sent her regrets when Roy invited her to visit Langtry. She thanked him for the honor and offered to pay for a town drinking fountain. Roy wrote back to tell her that "the only thing the citizens of Langtry did not drink was water."[3] Lily then sent him a set of silver-plated Colt Peacemakers. The judge treasured those pistols. He called his court to order by pounding on the bar with one of them.

Roy kept Lily's picture pinned to his wall, but the two never met. He saw her in person only once. In April 1888 he traveled to San Antonio to see Lily perform in *A Wife's Peril*. Roy wore his best clothes and paid top dollar for a front row seat. After the play his courage failed him. Would Lily want to see him? Unsure of himself, Roy turned shy. He left the theater without calling on her. Back home in Langtry he held a week-long fiesta to celebrate his big night.[4]

Roy named his saloon for actress Lily Langtry, the great love of his life. Lily, in turn, was charmed by his devotion. Although the two exchanged letters, they never met.

7
THE CLEANEST DOCKET IN TEXAS

Legend says that Roy named himself to the post of Justice of the Peace. The fact is, he held the post legally. In 1884 he had run for election and easily won a new term. Two years later he lost to John Gilcrease by eight votes, 17–25. Never one to give up, Roy pulled some strings. The commissioners of Val Verde County responded. They named him the JP for a new district that covered a vast area west of the Pecos. Secure in his post, Roy won the next four elections in a row.

In 1896 Jesus Torres entered the race. The town founder won, but Roy refused to give up the seal of office. In time the two JPs worked out a compromise. Roy tried cases and served as coroner north of the tracks. Torres handled court business and did the coroner's work on the south side. Whenever someone died both men raced to take charge.

Roy lost to Torres again in 1898, but then he made a comeback. He beat his old foe in 1900 and 1902. The Jersey Lilly was still in business.

Roy Bean never wore the black robes of a big city judge. He held court dressed in an ill-fitting suit. A sweat-stained bandanna hid the rope burn on his neck. By the time he was sixty, his hair and beard had turned gray. No longer slim and graceful, he carried 190 pounds on his 5-foot 10-inch frame. Despite his rumpled looks,

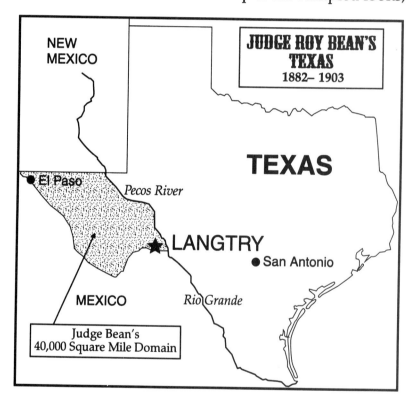

Judge Roy Bean was not kidding when he called himself "the Law West of the Pecos." For years lawmen in the vast territory brought their prisoners to Langtry for trial.

no one laughed at him. Just because he had never hung anyone did not mean that he would not pass a death sentence.

Roy started each court session by replacing his apron with a coat. That simple act turned the barroom into a courtroom. The judge sat behind the counter, his pistols close at hand. If lawyers were present, they used whiskey barrels as desks. The jury found seats on scattered boxes and barrels. When the weather was good, Roy sometimes moved his court outside to the porch.

Once a trial started Roy called numerous recesses. During those breaks the judge put on his apron again. He expected everyone—lawyers, prisoners, witnesses, and jury members—to buy a drink or two. On one occasion a lawyer paid for a 35-cent beer with a $10 gold eagle. When Bartender Bean shortchanged him, the lawyer let fly with a string of curses. That was all Judge Bean needed to hear. He fined the man $10.00 for disturbing the peace. "The beer is on me," he added.[1]

The locals counted their change with care. They knew that Roy often shortchanged his customers. His favorite victims were train passengers. The trick was to hold the money until the warning whistle blew. Afraid they would be left behind, the passengers would scurry off without their change.

The 1879 *Revised Statutes of Texas* served as Roy's one and only law book. "They send me a new book every year or so," he once remarked. "But I use it to light fires

This diorama of the Jersey Lilly's main room shows the bar, card tables, and wood-burning stove. Roy stands behind the bar, serving drinks under his prized picture of Lily Langtry. When court was in session, the bar became his judge's bench.

with."[2] The old book shows the marks of his pen. The penal code's comments about rustling are heavily underlined. Roy also kept a handwritten "Statoot Book." One entry says that cheating at cards is "a hanging offense, if ketched."[3]

Roy had little patience with lawyers and legal language. Once a lawyer said that he was going to *habeas corpus* the accused. He meant that the court had not shown proper cause for holding his client. Judge Bean ignored the legal issue. He turned on the lawyer and threatened to hang him for using "bad language" in his court.[4]

A JP's duties did not stop with holding court. As coroner, Judge Bean was paid five dollars to determine the cause of any sudden death. It was as coroner that Roy rode fifteen miles on muleback to the Pecos high bridge. Ten men had been crushed by falling timbers. Seven were dead. Three were badly hurt. Roy looked them over and winced at the thought of repeating that rough ride. Then he pronounced all ten men dead by accident. "Them three fellers is bound to die," he explained.[5]

Sometime in the 1890s a man told Roy that he had found a corpse. The man tried to describe the place where it lay, but Roy cut him off. He said he knew where the body was. "I rule that this *hombre* met his death by being shot by a person unknown who was a damn good shot," he said. The dead man, it turned out, had a bullet hole in the forehead.[6] Was Roy the "person unknown"? No one can say for sure.

What is certain is that Roy never passed up a chance to make a buck. For example, a strong wind once blew a man off a nearby railroad bridge. Coroner Bean found $40 and a pistol on the body. Solemnly he fined the corpse $40 for carrying a concealed weapon. He also kept the gun.

A visitor once asked Roy if he kept a record of his cases.

"No," he replied. "I have got the cleanest docket in the state of Texas. Not a scratch of the pen on it."[7]

8
A VISIT TO THE JERSEY LILLY

From 1885 on, Judge Bean reigned as a national hero. Newspapers and dime novels printed colorful accounts of his life. Some writers took liberties with the facts, but Roy did not mind. He enjoyed his years in the spotlight.

A rickety wooden porch ran across the front of the Jersey Lilly. Visitors who turned left could buy canned goods and sugar in the general store. They were more likely to veer right, attracted by the 15 x 30-foot saloon. A large pool table stood in the center of the room. Straw covered the floor. Roy could sometimes be found sleeping on the pool table. A central hall led to the Bean family's living quarters. An L-shaped wing held sleeping rooms that Roy rented by the night.

Over the years Roy's sons and daughters moved in with him. The children were sure that Roy adored them, despite his rough tongue. If his daughters hid to escape his wrath, he sometimes went looking for them with a shotgun. "I ought to kill 'em," he would yell. The whole town knew the gun was never loaded.[1]

Only Sam, Zulema, and Laura spent much time in school. When they grew up the girls married and moved to New Orleans. John became a ranch hand. Roy, Jr., found work with the railroad. Faithful Sam stayed home and worked in the Jersey Lilly. He lived to bury his father, then died in a barroom brawl.[2]

At the Jersey Lilly customers were seldom right. Roy often fined patrons 90 cents for not having change for a dollar. If he was not handing out fines, he cut corners in other ways. In summer he dunked a chunk of glass in

Along with his duties as judge, Roy served as Langtry's coroner. He often drove this two-wheeled buggy when called out to certify the cause of death. Roy did not look forward to those long, bone-jarring trips.

the mixed drinks to give the illusion that they were iced. In winter he burned a candle in the iron stove. The tiny flame, he argued, made people think the stove was putting out heat.[3]

Roy saved his "special whiskey" for patrons who complained that their drinks were weak. "Oh, you want pure pizen, do you?" the judge would snarl. Then he would pour from a jar in which dead tarantulas floated. One look cut off most complaints. Legend says that one foolish cowhand drank the "pizen"—and promptly dropped dead.[4]

The rascally judge was only one of the Jersey Lilly's attractions. Tourists also came by to visit Roy's zoo. The pens held coyotes, wolves, armadillos, snakes, and a mountain lion. Bruno, the black bear Roy kept chained to the porch, was the star. People loved to see the bear drink beer. When handed a bottle, Bruno pulled the cork with his teeth. Then he sat back and downed the beer in one long swallow. Bruno's bottomless thirst helped keep beer sales high.

Roy usually dressed like one of the tramps who begged drinks in his bar. To greet an important guest he would put on a formal coat and a top hat. One such time was the day in 1890 that railroad owner Jay Gould came through town. As Roy liked to tell his friends, "This Gould fellah, he's smart enough to make a livin' right here in Langtry."[5]

The fact that Gould's train was not scheduled to stop

Bruno, Judge Bean's pet bear, was the star of the Jersey Lilly's zoo. Visitors loved to see Bruno gulp down a bottle of beer. Drunks and wife-beaters were less fond of Bruno. They reformed quickly when Roy ordered them tied just out of Bruno's reach.

at Langtry did not bother Roy. He met the train at the station, waving his red bandanna. Alarmed by the sight of the danger signal, the engineer slammed on the brakes. When Gould looked out of his window Roy strolled over and shook hands. Minutes later the millionaire and his daughter were relaxing in the Jersey Lilly. His guests sat spellbound as Roy told them his best stories.

Two hours later the station telegraph clicked out a message. "Where was Gould? His train was two hours late." Rumors of his death were sweeping the stock market. The station agent smiled as he tapped out the reply. Gould, he reported, was drinking champagne and eating cookies with Judge Roy Bean.[6]

37

9
THE JERSEY LILLY
LIVES ON

The Jersey Lilly burned down in 1898. Judge Bean re-built, but on a smaller scale. The new one-room building was only 18 x 14 feet. To make room for the pool table, Roy added a lean-to. He was over seventy now and content to cut back on his work load. He was always ready to perform a five-dollar wedding, however.

To add drama Roy paraded the bride and groom around the barroom. As he finished the ceremony, he would ask the couple to hold up their right hands. Then Roy's deep voice would fill the room. "By the authority of the Constitution of the United States, the great State of Texas, and the Law West of the Pecos, I, Roy Bean, Justice of the Peace of this district, hereby pronounce you man and wife." Then he would add a phrase more often heard at hangings: "May God have mercy on your souls."[1]

Roy also took it on himself to grant divorces. When that news reached El Paso, a District Court judge hurried to Langtry. The judge warned Roy he had no legal right to divorce people.

Roy only shrugged. "Well, I married 'em, so I figure I've got the right to rectify my errors," he explained.[2]

March 1903 was an exciting time for the old man. Lily Langtry had promised to visit him during her upcoming tour. But even as Roy planned her welcome, his health was failing. He fell deathly ill during a trip to San Antonio. Hard living and hard liquor had taken their toll. Judge Bean died on March 16 with a circle of friends standing by.

After Roy died in 1903 his children took his body to Del Rio for burial. He lies beneath a simple tombstone, next to his son Sam.

39

Sam, Zulema, and Laura took their father's body to Del Rio, Texas. The Langtry cemetery, they reasoned, was filled with men who had died violent deaths. Above his grave they placed a simple marker. It reads:

JUDGE ROY BEAN
Justice of the Peace
Law West of the Pecos

Ten months later Lily Langtry climbed the wooden steps to the Jersey Lilly. The actress found the saloon just as Roy had left it. She cut a deck of cards for luck. Someone gave her one of the judge's pistols. The visit over, Lily returned to her sleeping car. A rowdy bunch of cowboys fired their guns in the air as the train pulled away.

Today, Roy lives on as one of the legends of the Wild West. He was a rascal to be sure, but he was a brave, clever rascal. By sheer strength of will, he brought law and order to a land that knew little of either.

A few Roy Bean stories do not hold up to the facts. Roy has been called a "hanging judge," but he never hanged anyone. He loved to threaten culprits with hanging, but he always let them escape. Once in a while he let the punishment fit the crime. To reform a wife-beater, he chained the terrified man inches from Bruno's outstretched claws.

It is true that Roy shortchanged customers. It is true that he fined jurors for not drinking. The fact is, he was

The Jersey Lilly fell into disrepair after Roy's death. Today, thanks to the Texas Highway Department, the building has been rebuilt. The new Jersey Lilly attracts tourists from all over the globe.

part con man. Customers would have felt cheated if he had not played the rascal for them.

Today a visitors' center welcomes tourists to Langtry. The modern building dwarfs the old Jersey Lilly. Rebuilt and scrubbed clean, the tiny saloon stands in a cactus garden. Each year thousands stop by to pay their respects to the Law West of the Pecos.

NOTES BY CHAPTER

Chapter 1

1. Robert Casey, *The Texas Border* (Indianapolis, Ind.: Bobbs-Merrill Co., 1950), pp. 211–214.

2. Major Horace Bell, *On the Old West Coast* (New York: Arno Press, 1976), pp. 232–233.

Chapter 2

1. Dan Thrapp, *Encyclopedia of Frontier Biography* (Glendale, Calif.: Arthur Clark Co., 1988), p. 79, says Bean was born circa 1827.

2. Robert Elman, *Fired in Anger: The Personal Handguns of American Heroes and Villains* (Garden City, N.Y.: Doubleday, 1968), p. 288.

3. C. L. Sonnichsen, *Roy Bean: Law West of the Pecos* (Lincoln, Neb.: University of Nebraska Press, 1943), p. 16.

4. Jay Robert Nash, *Encyclopedia of World Crime* (Wilmette, Ill.: Crime Books, 1990), p. 288.

Chapter 3

1. Major Horace Bell, *On the Old West Coast* (New York: Arno Press, 1976), p. 227.

2. Robert Elman, *Fired in Anger: The Personal Handguns of American Heroes and Villains* (Garden City, N.Y.: Doubleday, 1968), p. 290.

3. C. L. Sonnichsen, *Roy Bean: Law West of the Pecos* (Lincoln, Neb.: University of Nebraska Press, 1943), p. 36.

4. Everett Lloyd, *Law West of the Pecos* (San Antonio: The Baylor Co., 1936), p. 42.

Chapter 4

1. C. L. Sonnichsen, *Roy Bean: Law West of the Pecos* (Lincoln, Neb.: University of Nebraska Press, 1943), p. 41.

2. Robert Elman, *Fired in Anger: The Personal Handguns of American Heroes and Villains* (Garden City, N.Y.: Doubleday, 1968), p. 290.

3. Sonnichsen, p. 44.

4. Elman, p. 291.

5. Sonnichsen, p. 64.

Chapter 5

1. C. L. Sonnichsen, *Roy Bean: Law West of the Pecos* (Lincoln, Neb.: University of Nebraska Press, 1943), pp. 66–68.

2. *San Antonio Express*, July 27, 1882.

3. Robert Casey, *The Texas Border* (Indianapolis, Ind.: Bobbs-Merrill Co., 1950), p. 203.

Chapter 6

1. C. L. Sonnichsen, *Roy Bean: Law West of the Pecos* (Lincoln, Neb.: University of Nebraska Press, 1943), pp. 93–94.

2. Jay Robert Nash, *Encyclopedia of World Crime* (Wilmette, Ill.: Crime Books, 1990), p. 289.

3. James L. Haley, *Texan: An Album of History* (Garden City, N.Y.: Doubleday, 1985), p. 242.

4. Nash, p. 289.

Chapter 7

1. Everett Lloyd, *Law West of the Pecos* (San Antonio: The Baylor Co., 1936), p. 70.

2. C. L. Sonnichsen, *Roy Bean: Law West of the Pecos* (Lincoln, Neb.: University of Nebraska Press, 1943), pp. 89–90.

3. James L. Haley, *Texan: An Album of History* (Garden City, N.Y.: Doubleday, 1985), p. 242.

4. Dan Thrapp, *Encyclopedia of Frontier Biography* (Glendale, Calif.: Arthur Clark Co., 1988), p. 79.

5. Sonnichsen, pp. 125–126.

6. Robert Elman, *Fired in Anger: The Personal Handguns of American Heroes and Villains* (Garden City, N.Y.: Doubleday, 1968), p. 293.

7. Myron W. Tracy, "Roy Bean: Law West of the Pecos," in J. Frank Dobie, ed., *Straight Texas* (Hatboro, Pa.: Folklore Associates, 1966), p. 114.

Chapter 8

1. C. L. Sonnichsen, *Roy Bean: Law West of the Pecos* (Lincoln, Neb.: University of Nebraska Press, 1943), p. 142.

2. Everett Lloyd, *Law West of the Pecos* (San Antonio: The Baylor Co., 1936), p. 46.

3. Sonnichsen, p. 146.

4. Ibid. p. 160.

5. Robert Casey, *The Texas Border* (Indianapolis, Ind.: Bobbs-Merrill Co., 1950), p. 205.

6. Ibid. p. 205.

Chapter 9

1. C. L. Sonnichsen, *Roy Bean: Law West of the Pecos* (Lincoln, Neb.: University of Nebraska Press, 1943), p. 116.

2. Major Horace Bell, *On the Old West Coast* (New York: Arno Press, 1976), p. 232.

GLOSSARY

bandanna—A square of cotton cloth cowboys wear around their necks to prevent sunburn. They also use bandannas to protect their faces during windstorms.

blockade—The use of warships and other military forces to cut off an opponent's trade and communications.

Camino Real—The network of roads that linked Mexico City with the outlying provinces. The name translates as "the Royal Highway."

Civil War—The war between the free Northern states and the slave-owning Southern States, 1861–1865.

Colt Peacemaker—A six-shot revolver that was popular in the Wild West.

coroner—A public official who looks into any death thought to be caused by other than natural causes.

dime novels—Low-cost magazines that printed popular fiction during the late 1800s.

docket—In a courtroom, *docket* has two meanings. It can be a list of the cases waiting to be heard by the court, or it can be a brief summary of the cases already decided.

gold eagle—A $10 gold coin that was popular in the Wild West.

habeas corpus—A writ of *habeas corpus* requires that the court release a suspect who is being held without proper cause.

Justice of the Peace (JP)—A public official who presides over the lowest level of county courts. Unlike Judge Roy Bean, modern justices of the peace handle only minor cases.

kerosene—A fuel oil used in lanterns and heating stoves. Kerosene is ill-tasting and poisonous if swallowed.

legend—A story that many people believe, but which is almost always untrue.

Mexican War—The war between the United States and Mexico, 1846–1848. Mexico was defeated and sold California and New Mexico territory to the United States for $15 million.

pontoon bridge—A temporary bridge held up by floating supports.

railhead—The farthest point to which railroad tracks have been laid.

tallow—The white, tasteless animal fat that was once used in cooking or as a lubricant.

tequila—A strong alcoholic beverage distilled from the agave, or century plant.

Texas Rangers—An elite force of Texas law enforcement officers.

MORE GOOD READING ABOUT JUDGE ROY BEAN

Bell, Major Horace. *On the Old West Coast.* New York: Arno Press, 1976.

Casey, Robert J. *The Texas Border.* Indianapolis, Ind.: Bobbs-Merrill Co., 1950, pp. 195–214.

Elman, Robert. *Fired in Anger: The Personal Handguns of American Heroes and Villains.* Garden City, N.Y.: Doubleday, 1968, pp. 285–296.

Haley, James L. *Texan: An Album of History.* Garden City, N.Y.: Doubleday, 1985, pp. 241–244.

Lloyd, Everett. *Law West of the Pecos.* San Antonio: The Baylor Co., 1936.

Sonnichsen, C. L. *Roy Bean: Law West of the Pecos.* Lincoln, Neb.: University of Nebraska Press, 1943.

Tracy, Myron W. "Roy Bean: Law West of the Pecos," in J. Frank Dobie, ed., *Straight Texas.* Hatboro, Pa.: Folklore Associates, 1966, pp. 111–119.

INDEX